desire

/dɪˈzʌɪə/

noun

1. 1.

a strong feeling of wanting to have something or wishing for something to happen.
"he resisted public desires for choice in education"

synonyms:
wish, want; More

-

verb

1. 1.

strongly wish for or want (something).
"he never achieved the status he so desired"

synonyms:
wish for, want, long for, yearn for, crave, set one's heart on, hanker after/for, pine for/after, thirst for, itch for, be desperate for, be bent on, have a need for, covet, aspire to;
have a fancy for, fancy, feel like, feel in need of;
informal have a yen for, yen for, be dying for
"they earnestly desired peace"
required, necessary, proper, right, correct;
appropriate, fitting, suitable, called for;
preferred, chosen, selected, expected
"the cloth is then cut to the desired length"
wished for, wanted;
sought-after, longed for, yearned for, craved, pined for, needed, coveted
"the ruling party is able to manipulate the economy for the desired results on election day"

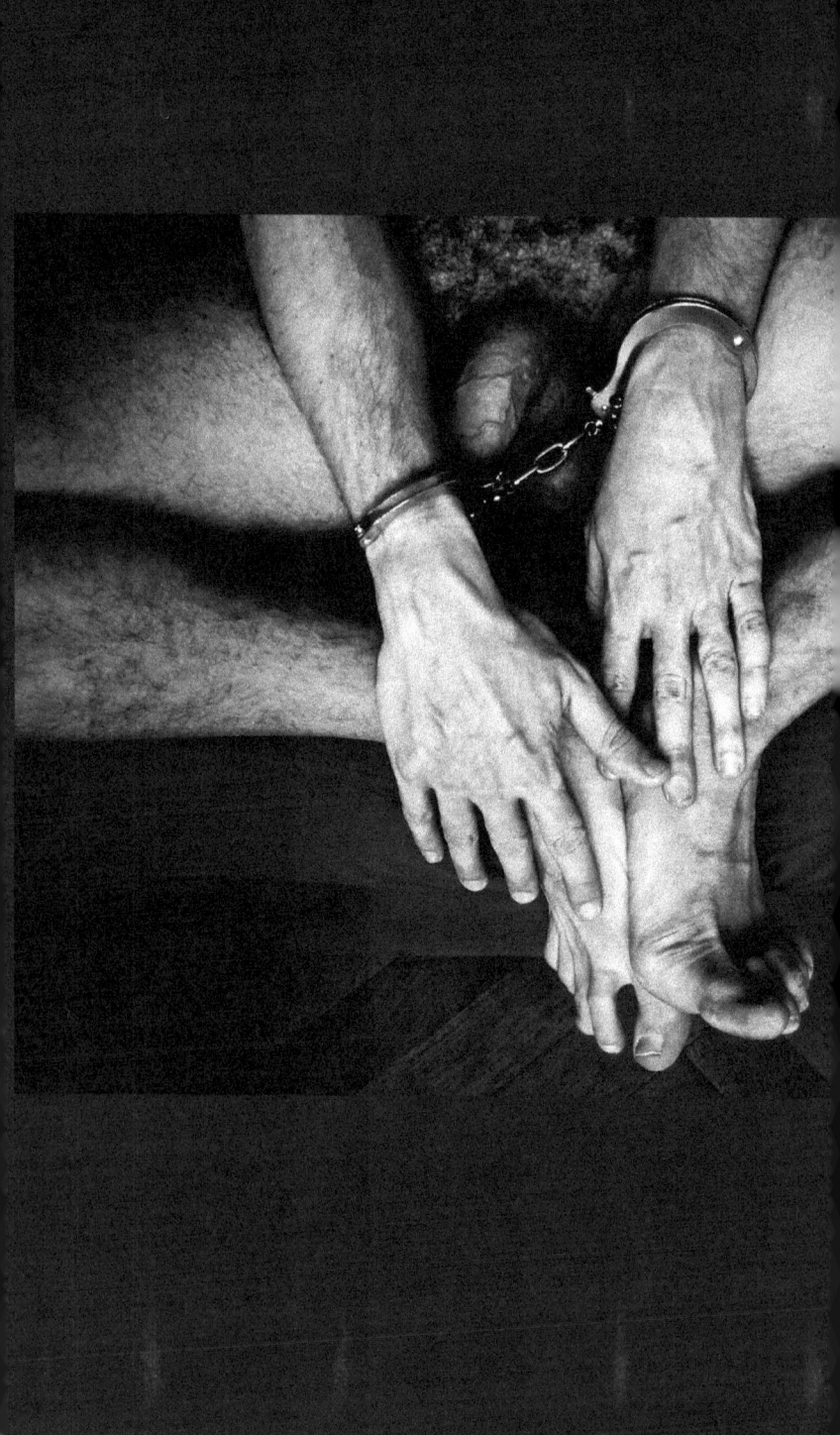

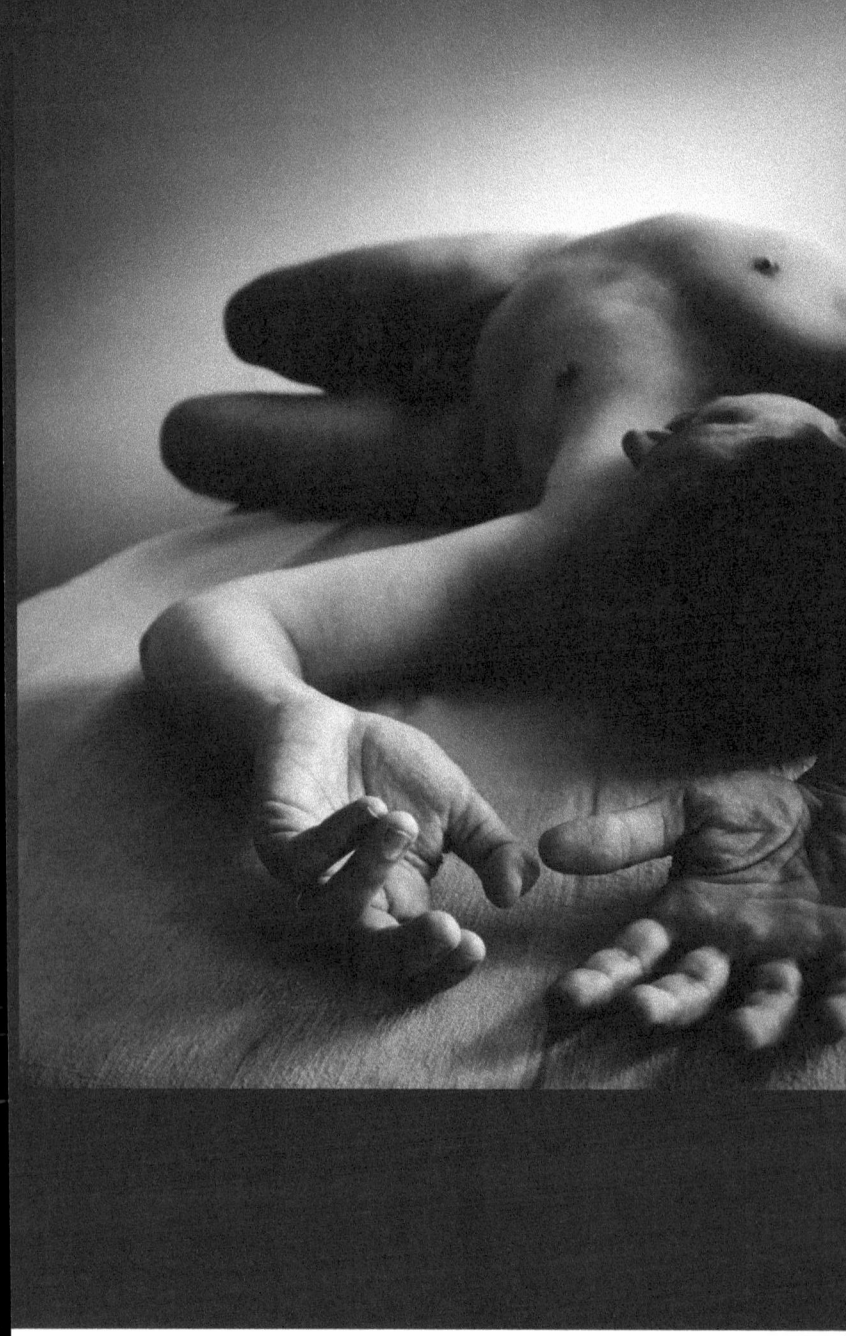

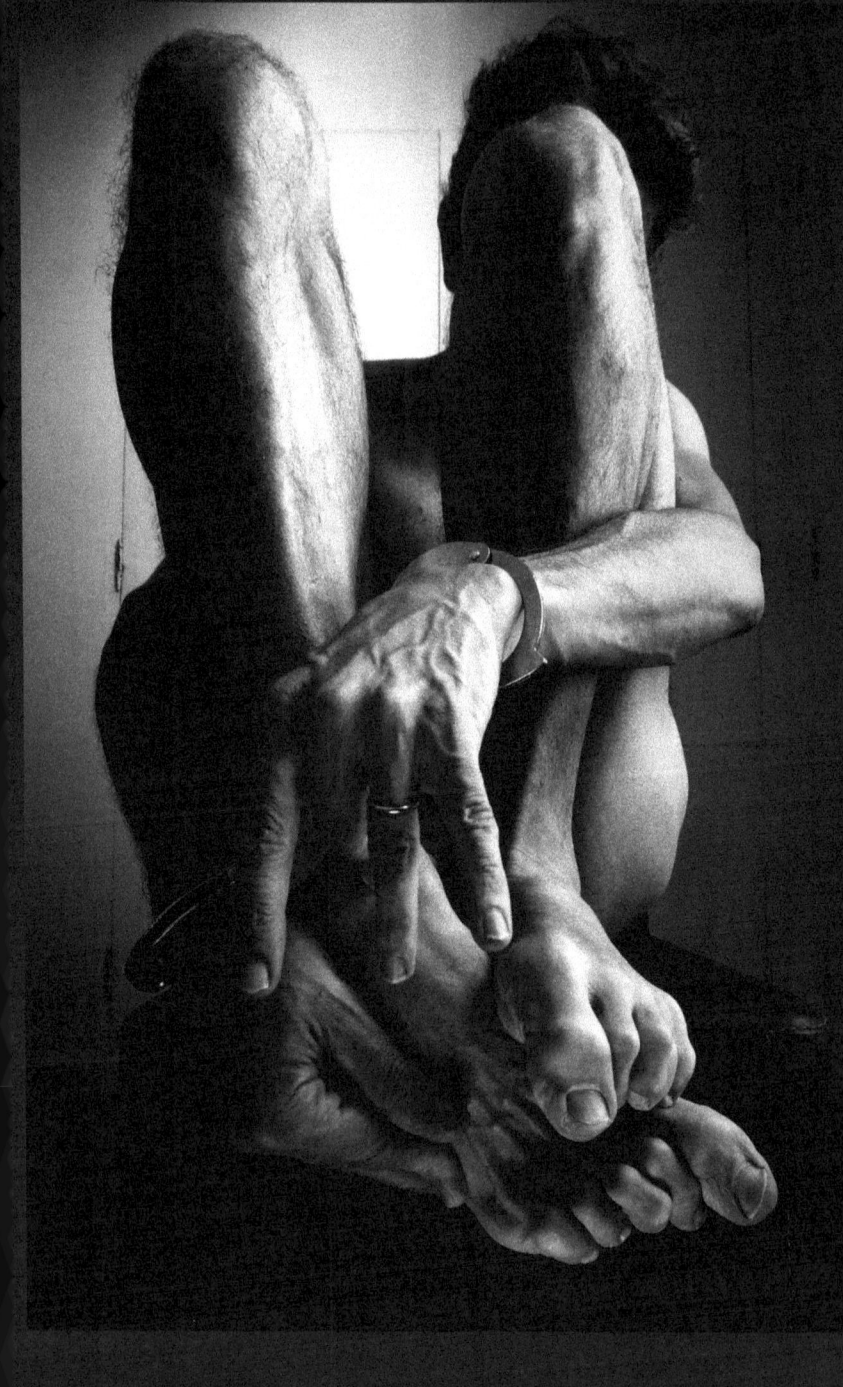

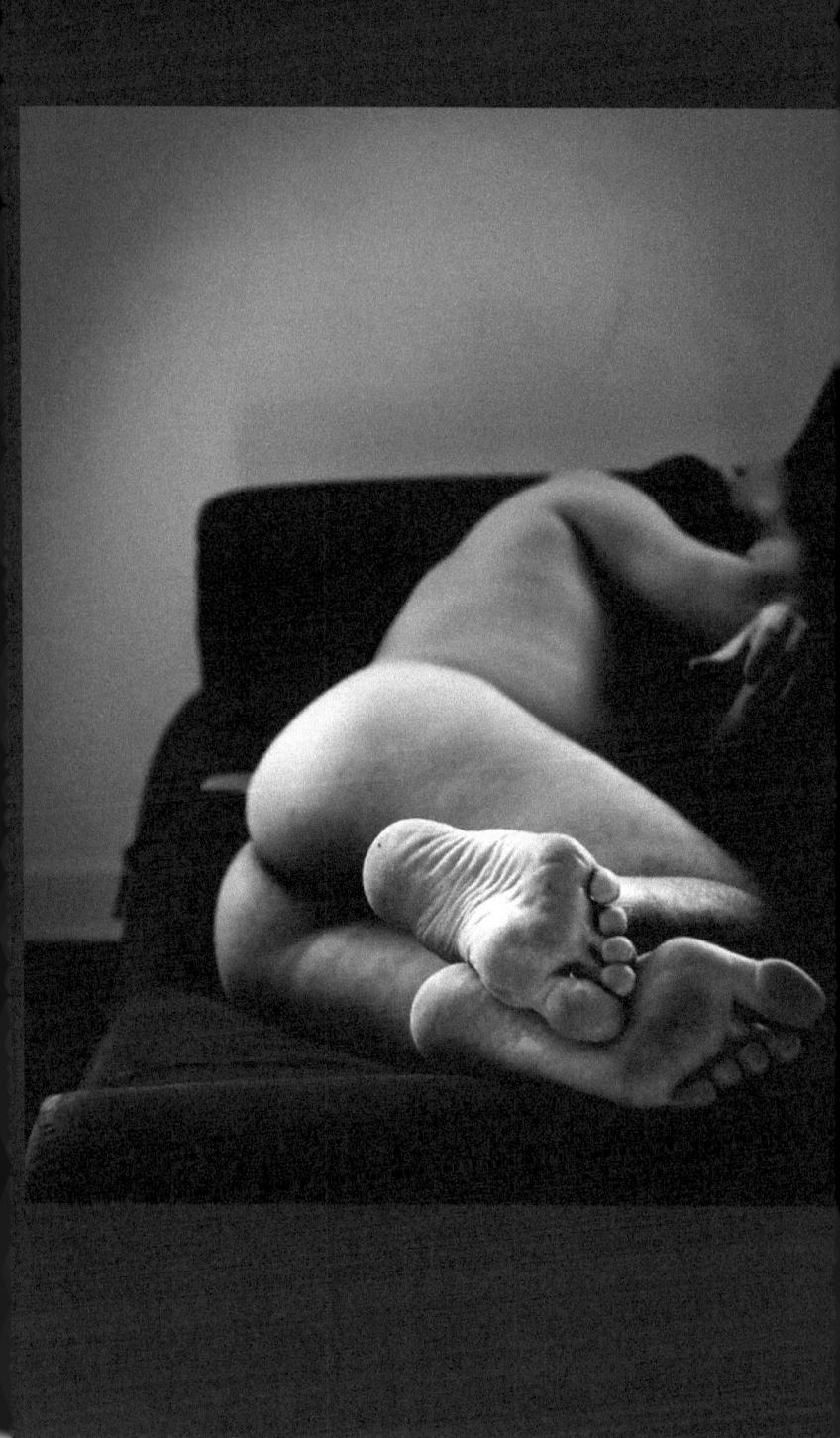

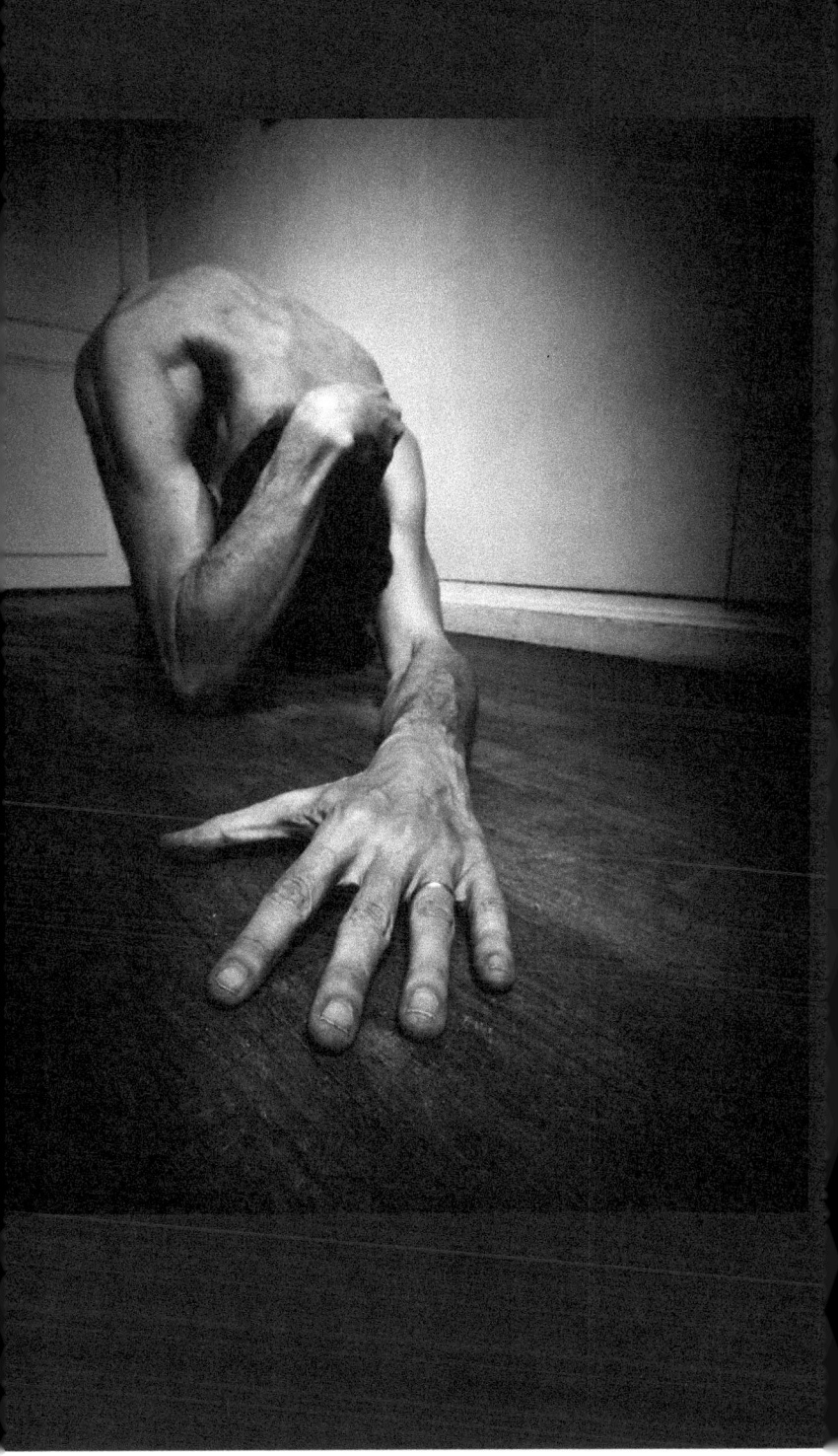

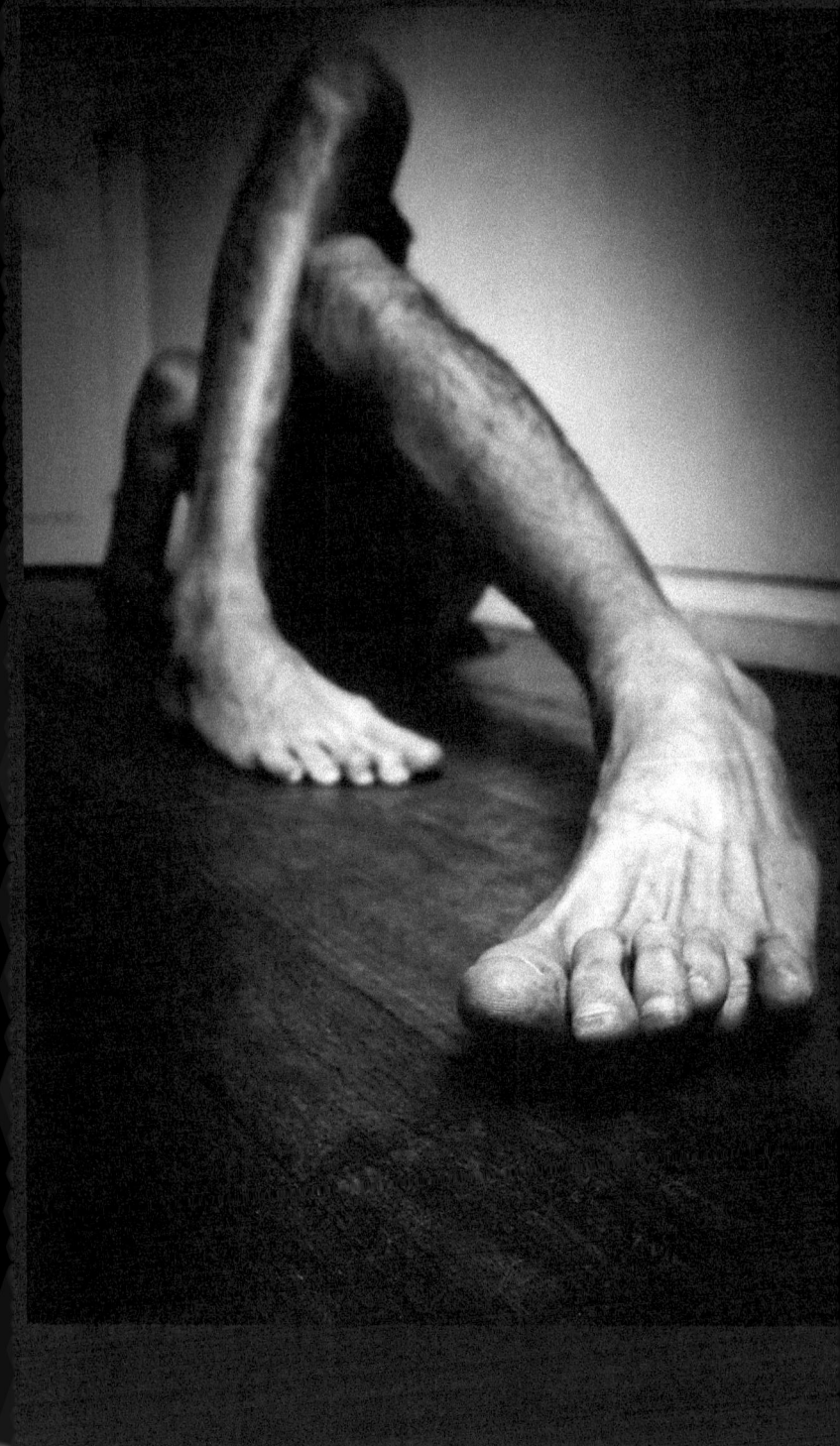

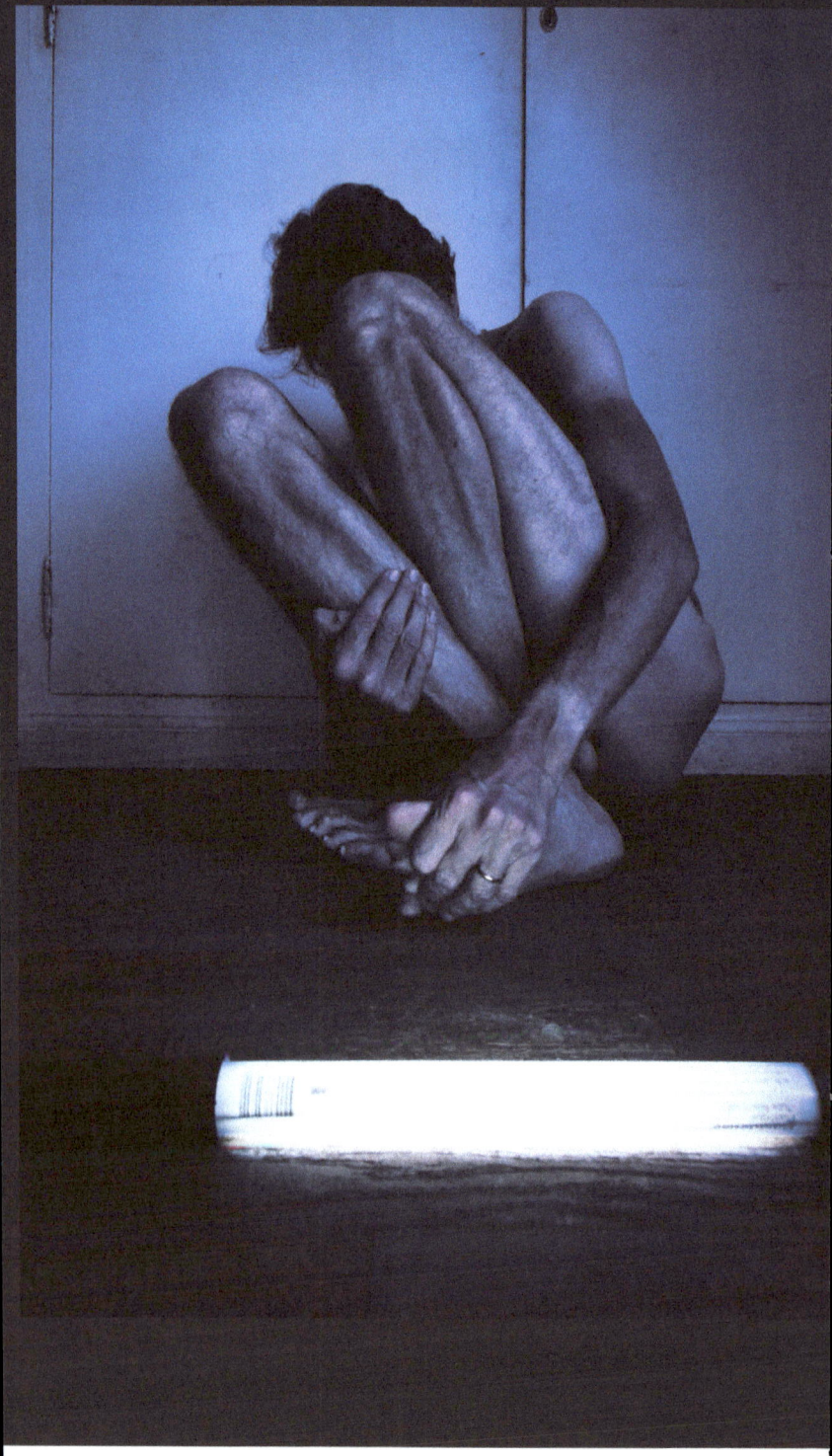

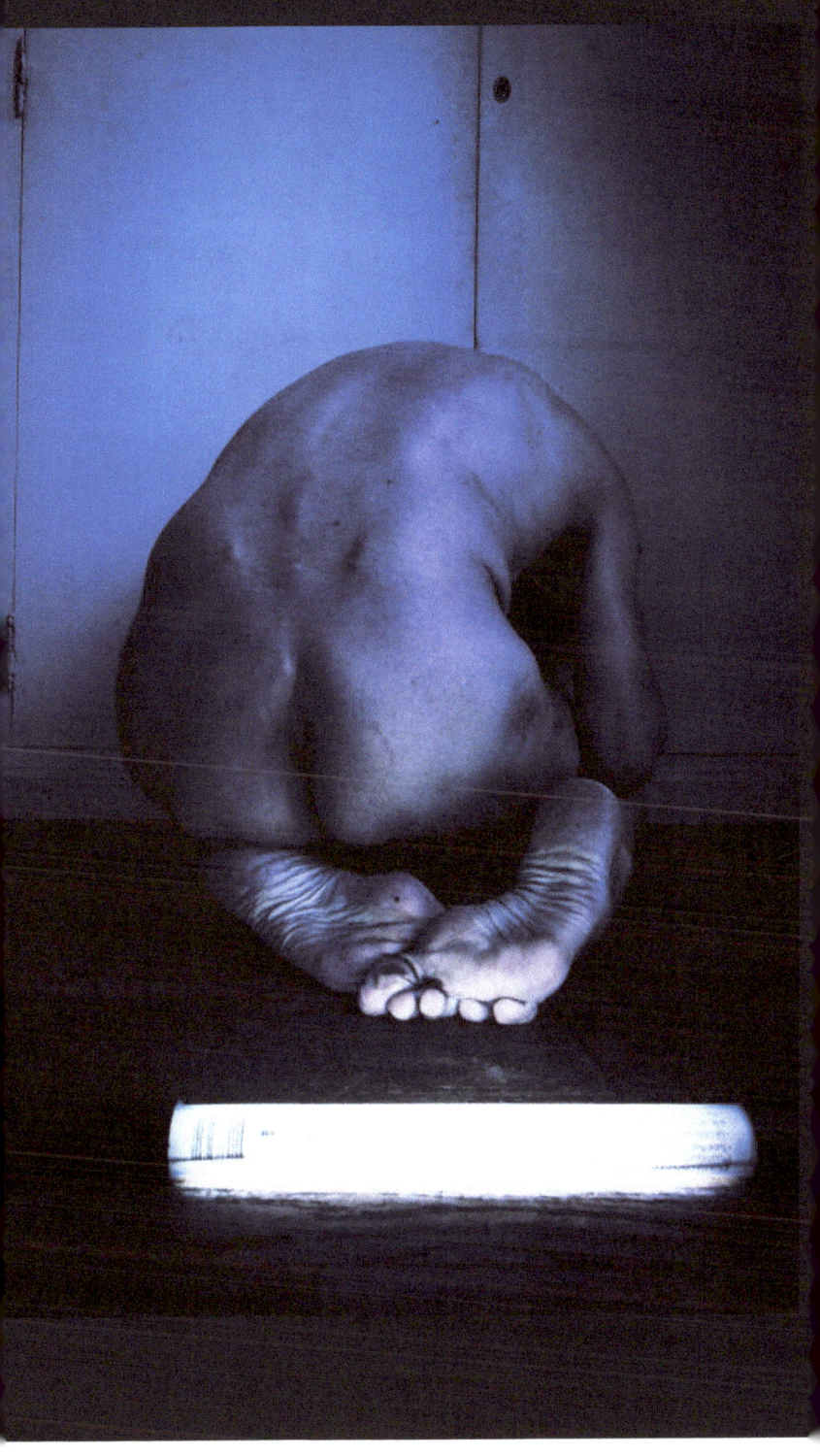

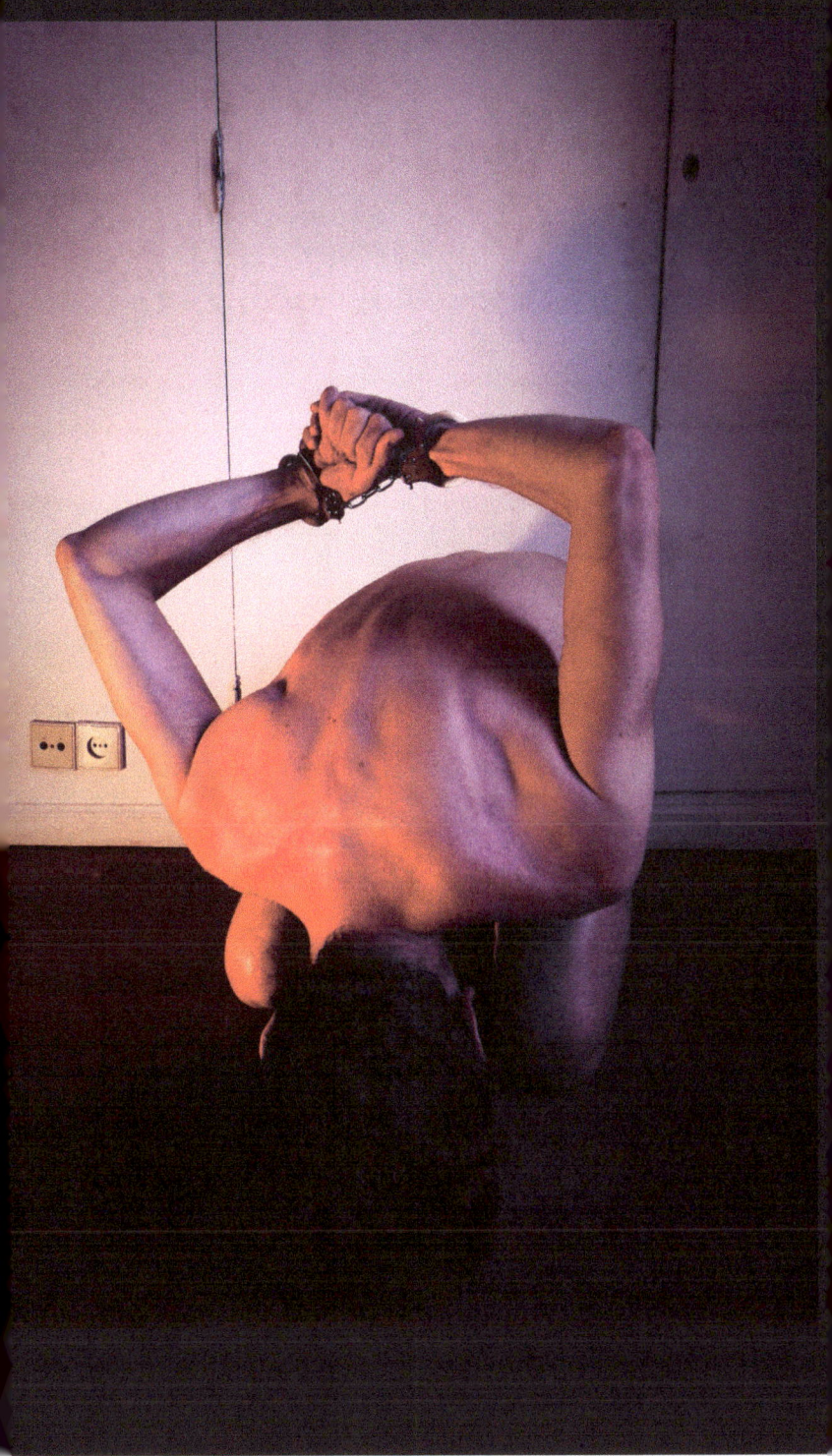

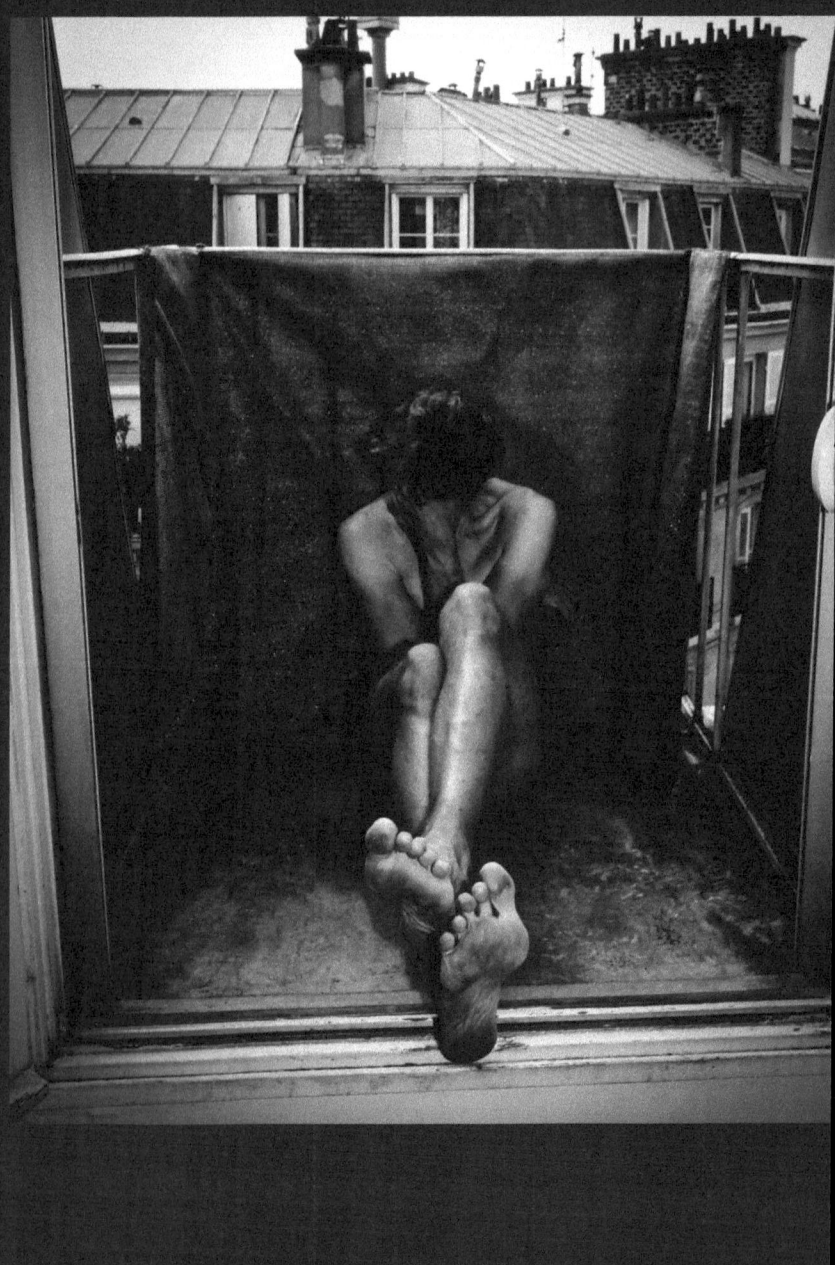

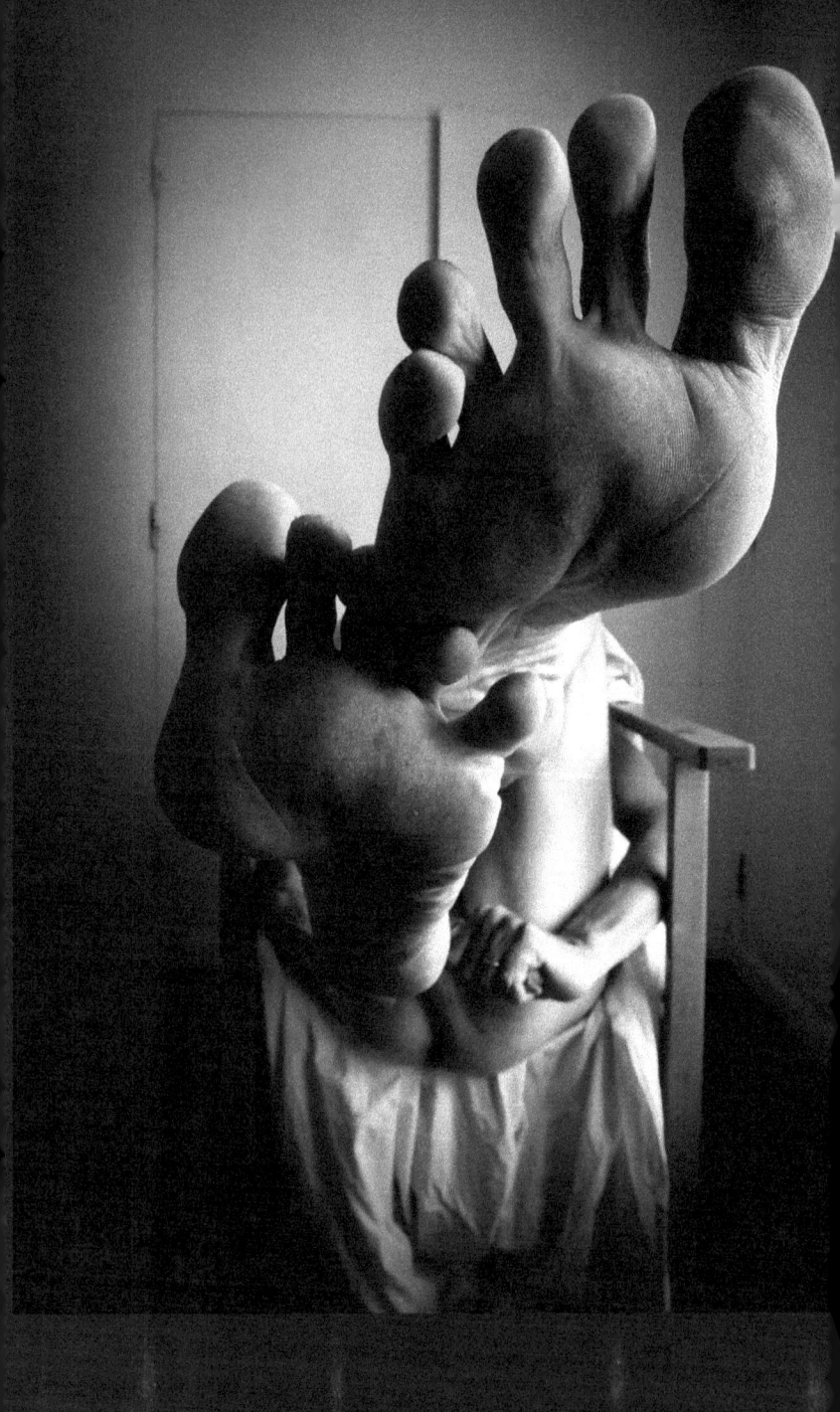

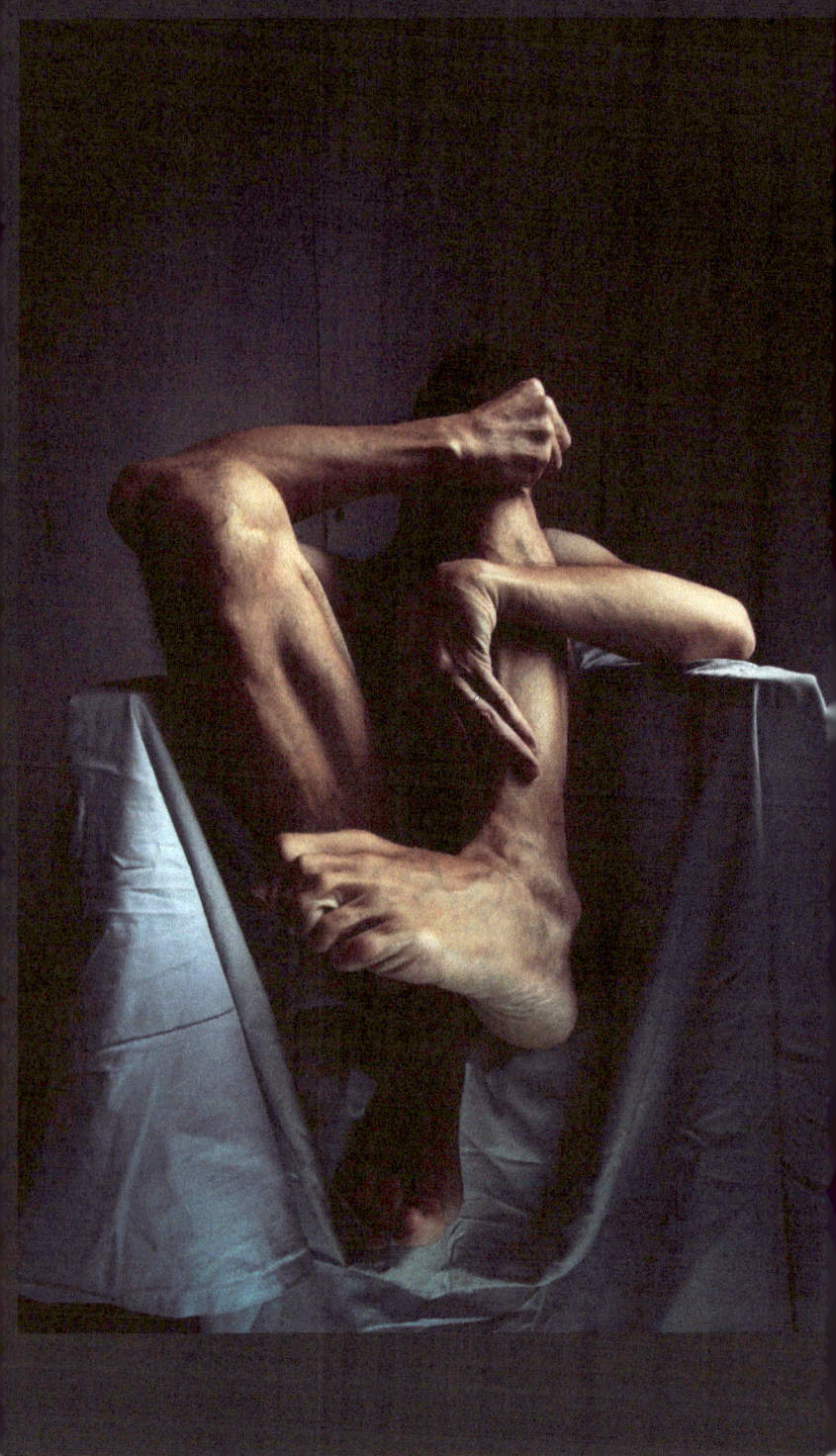

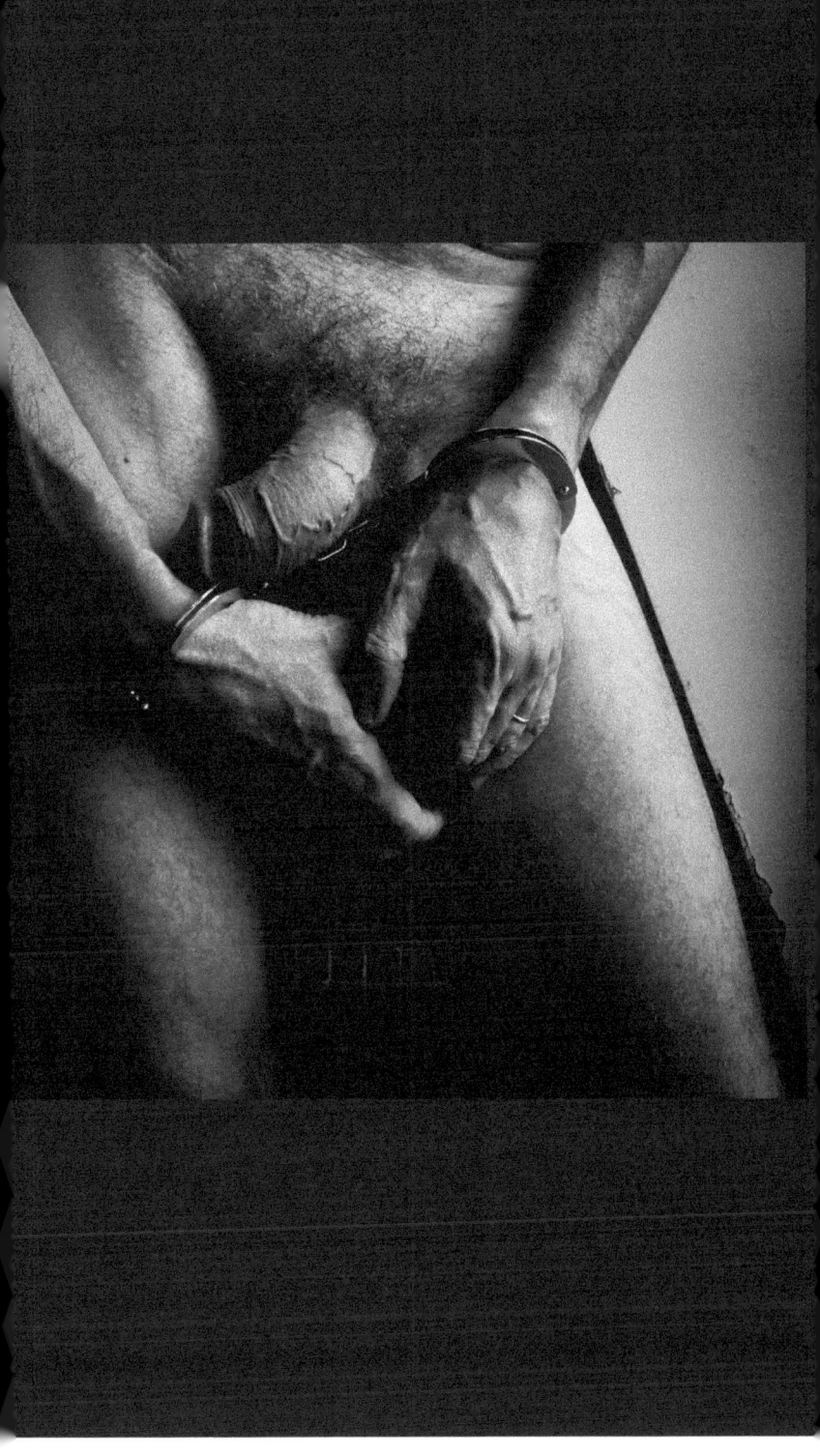

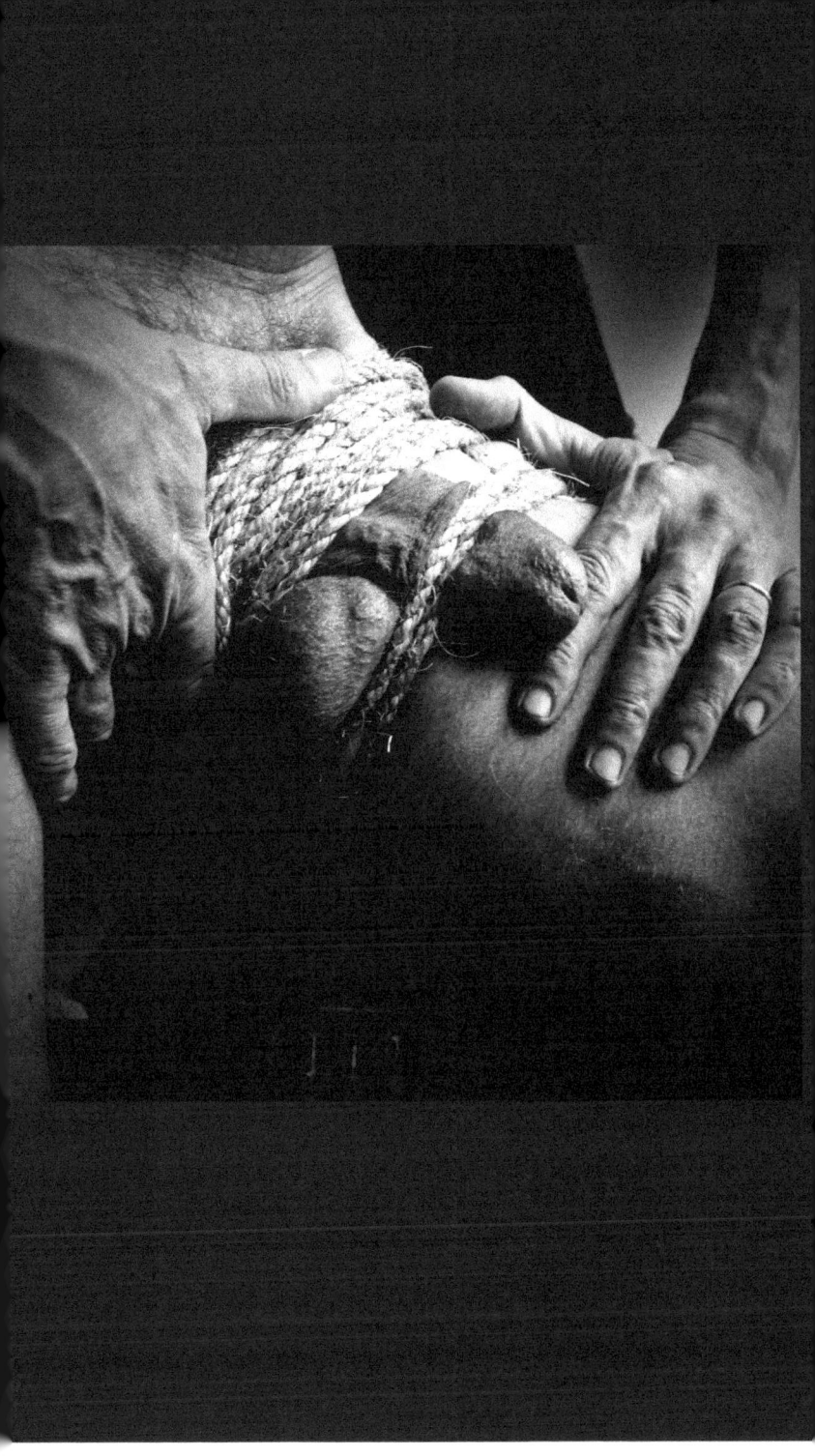

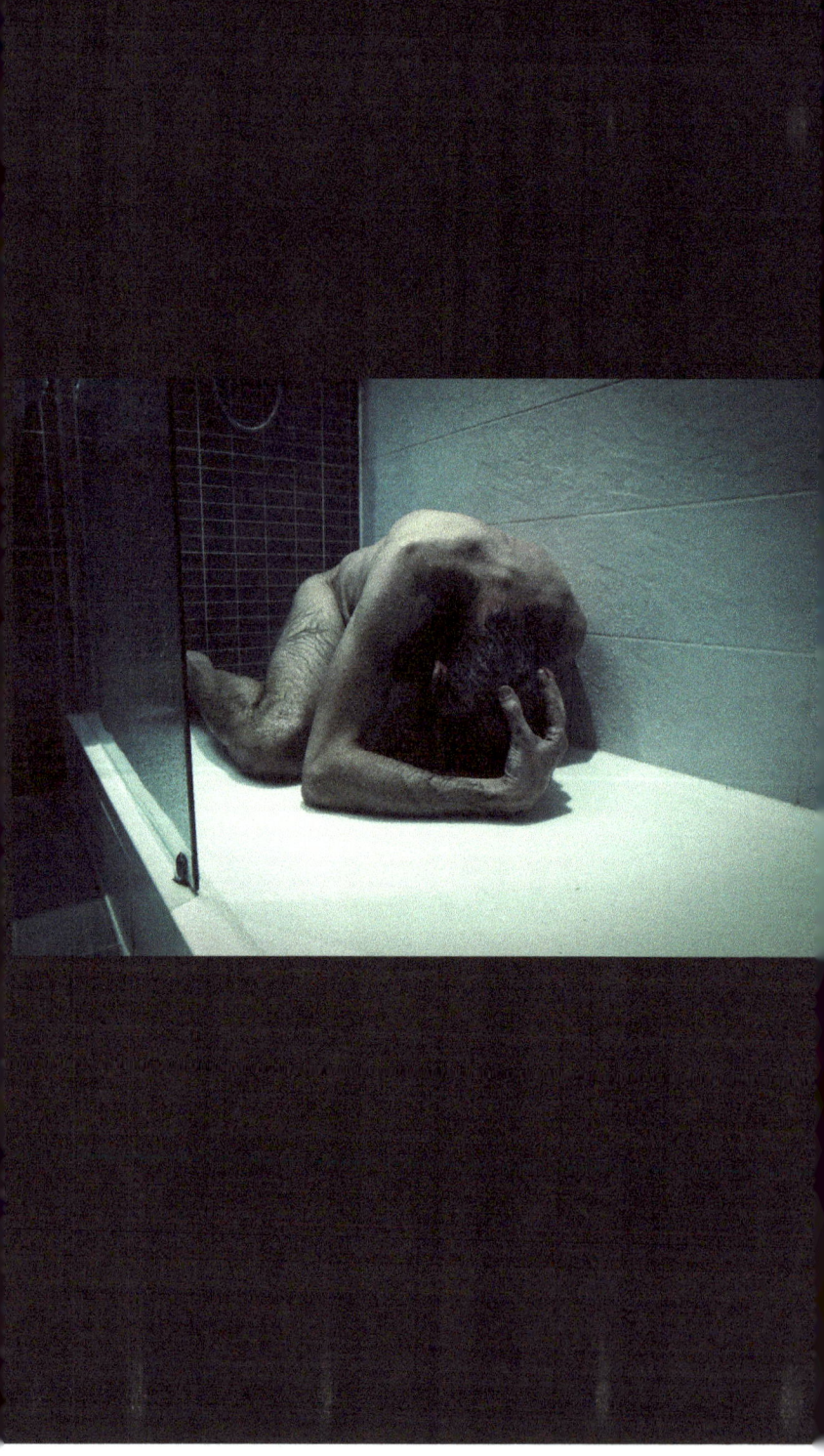

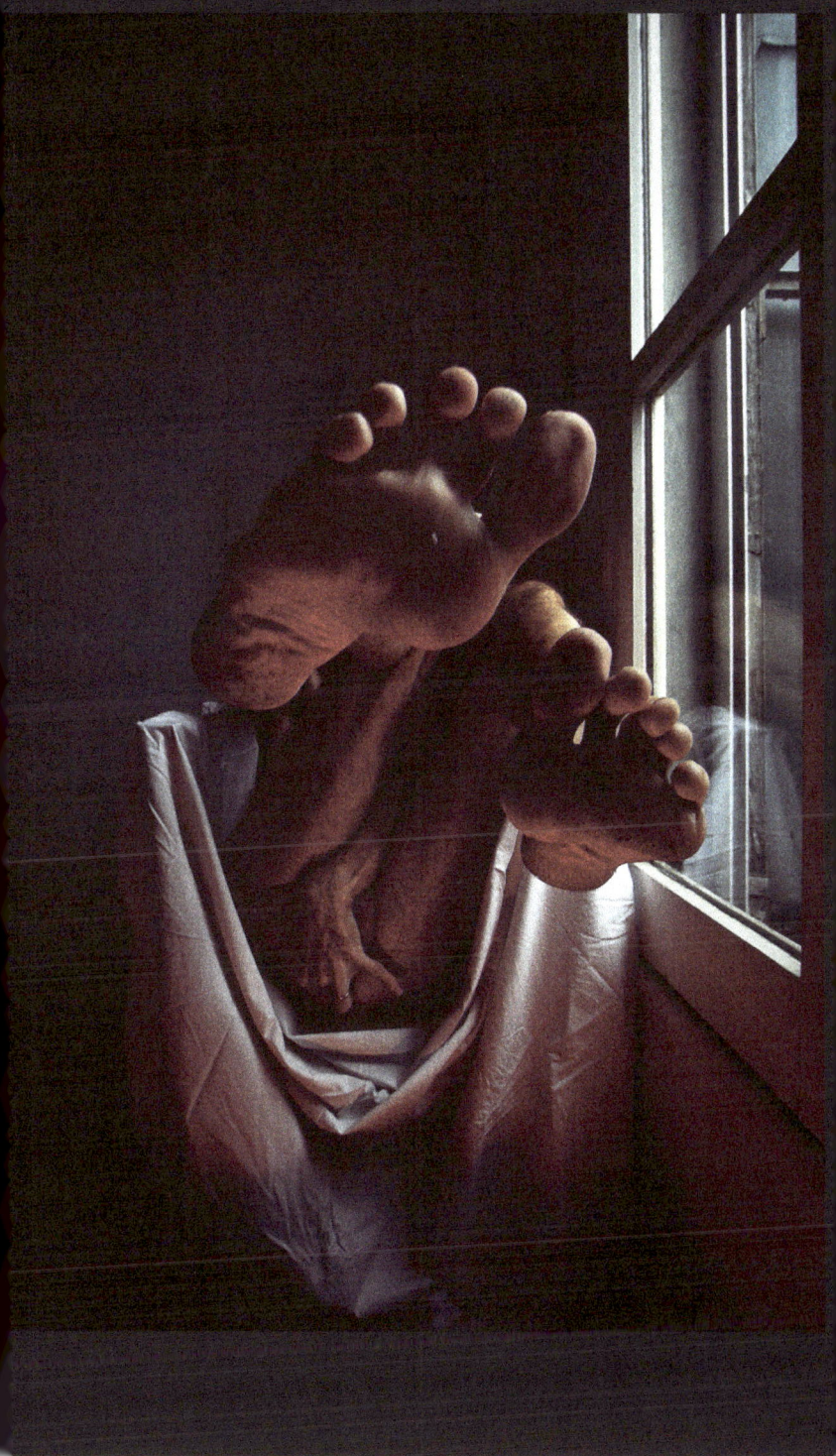

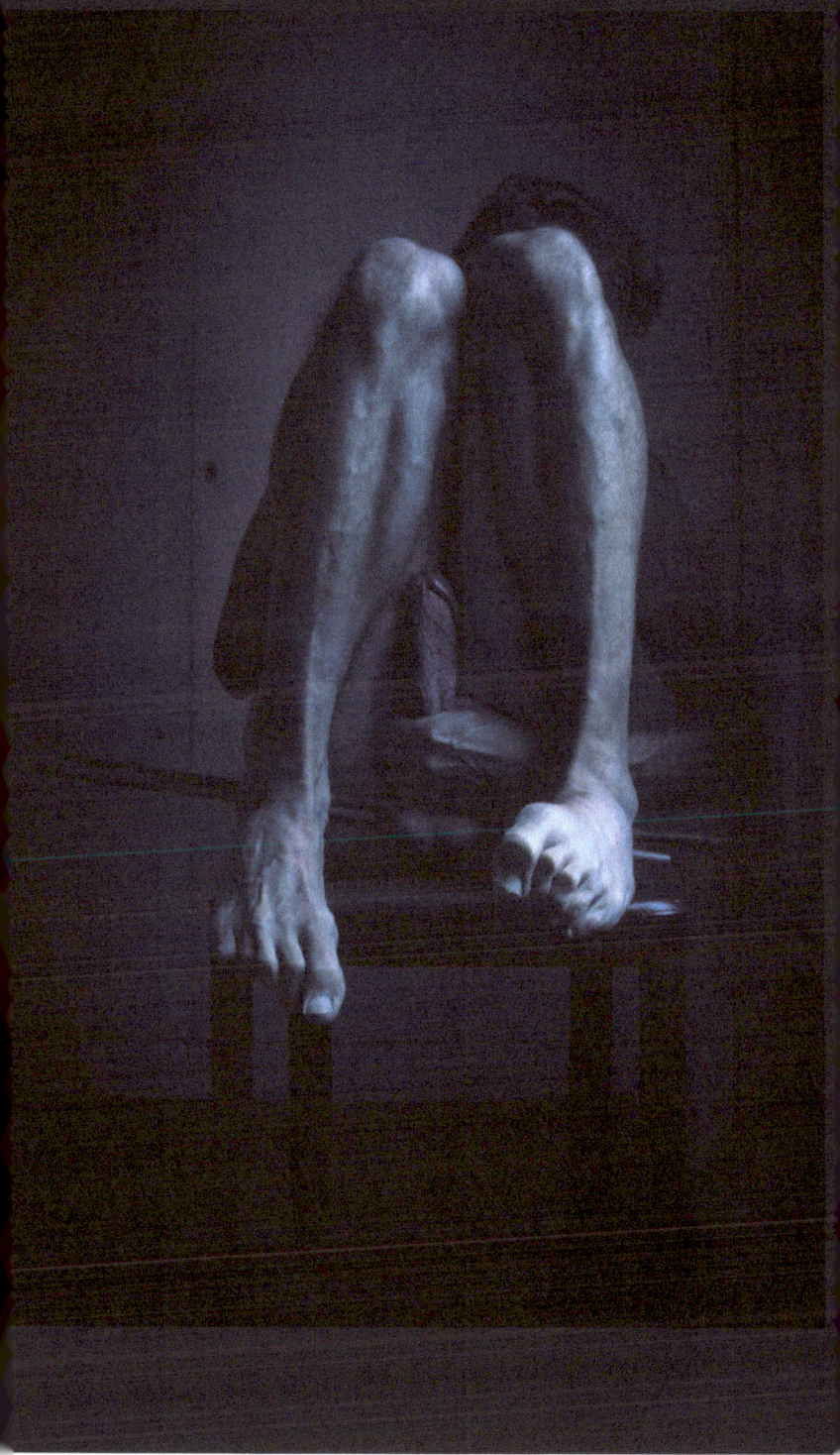

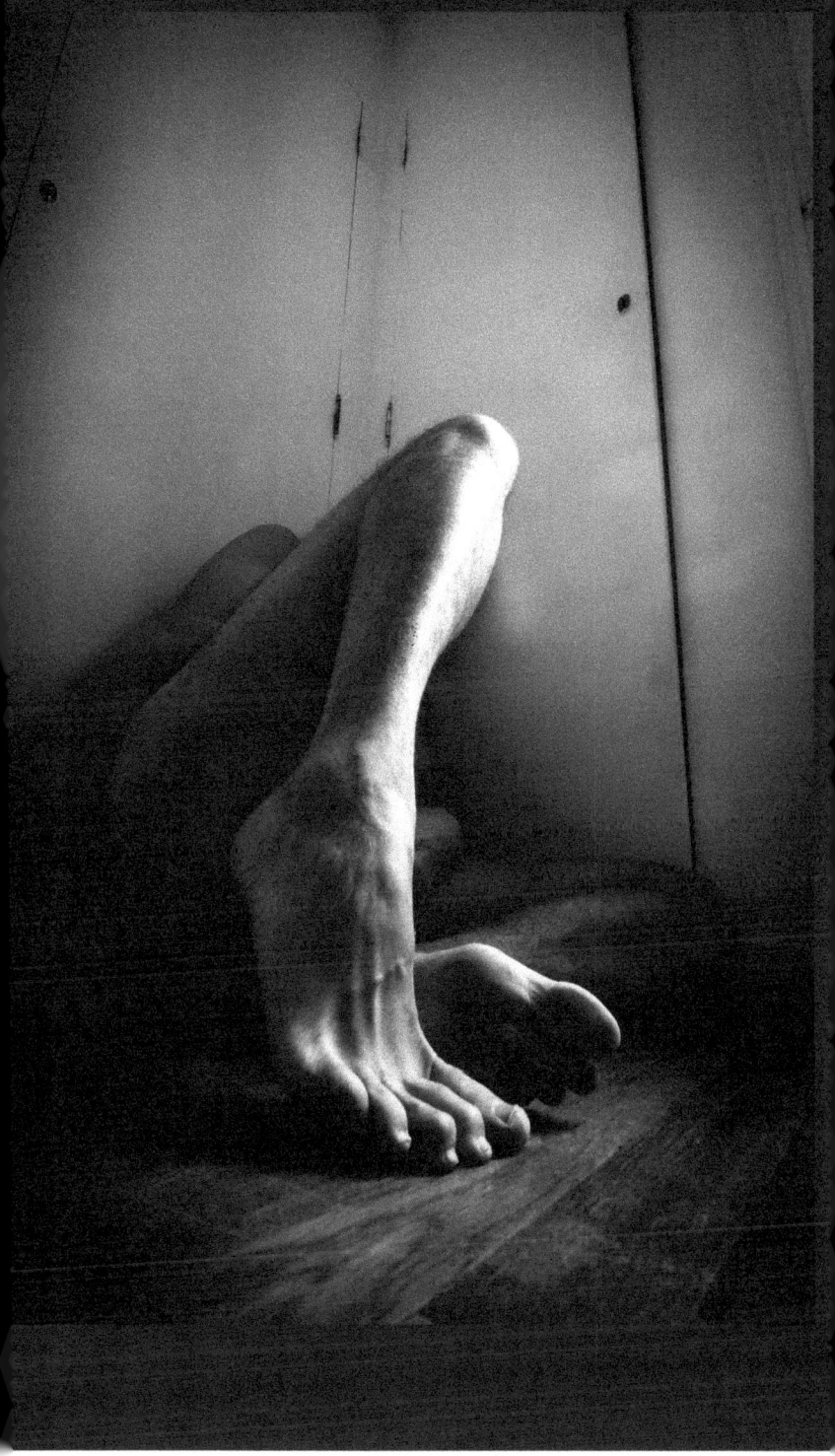

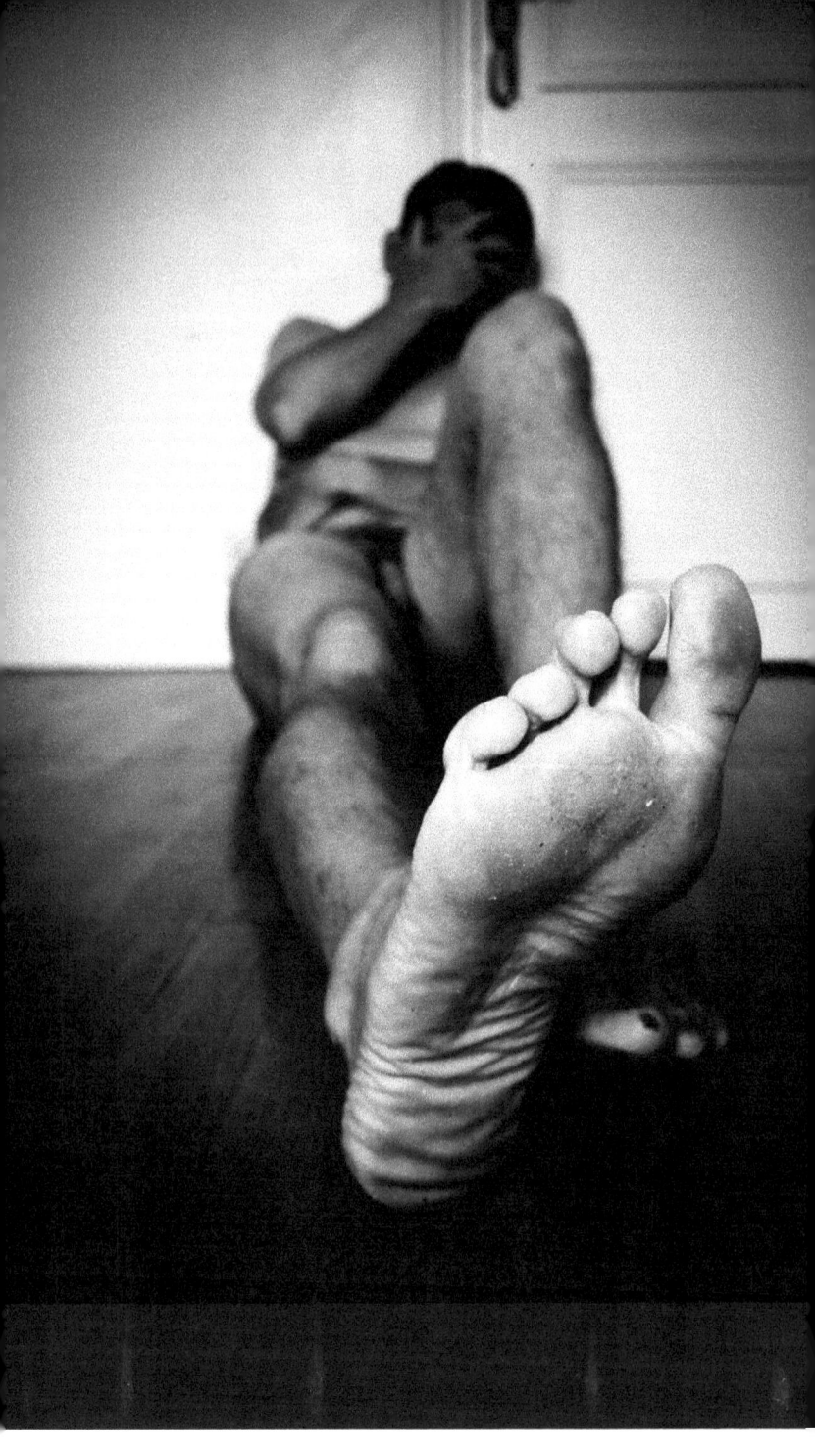

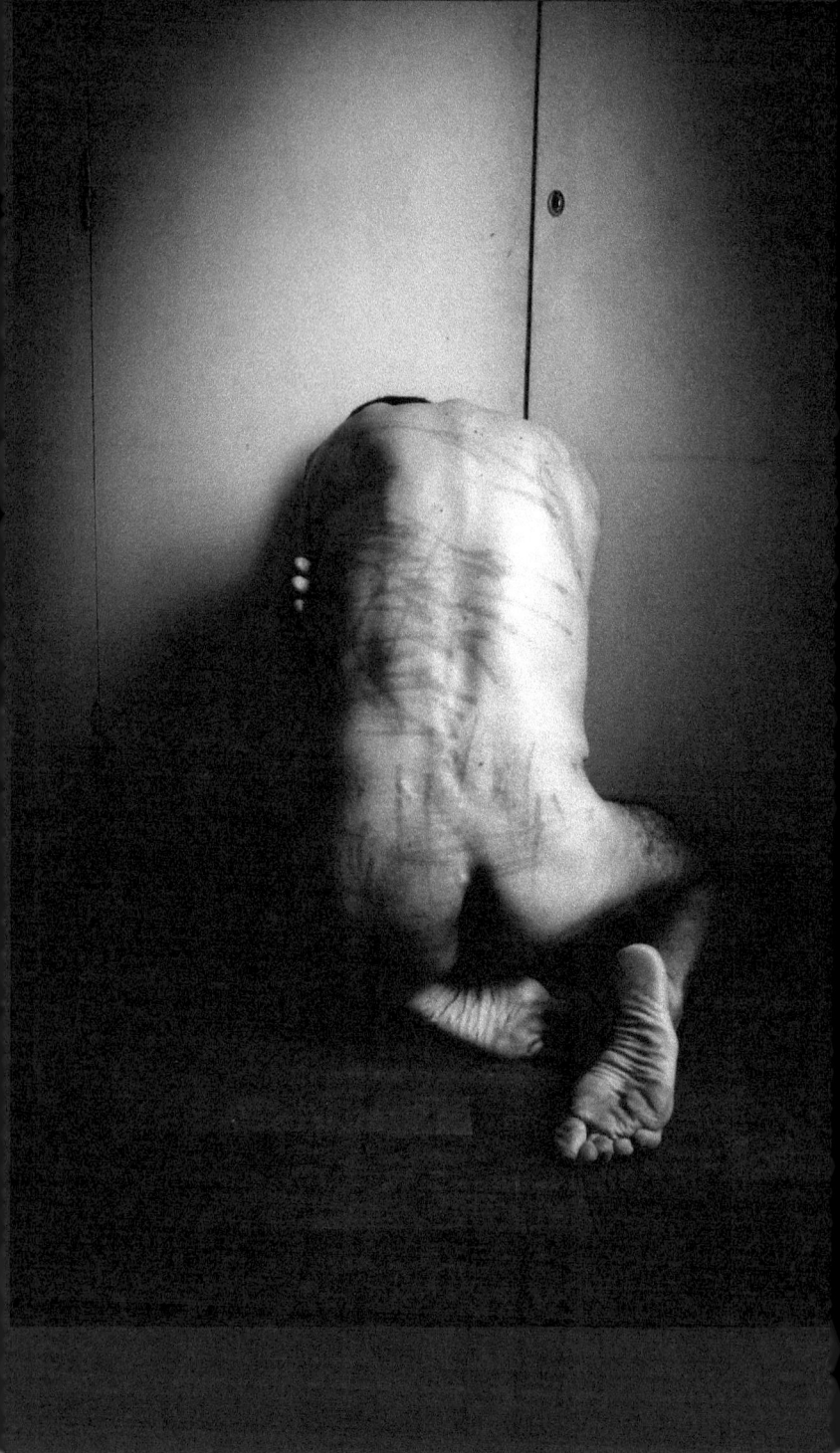

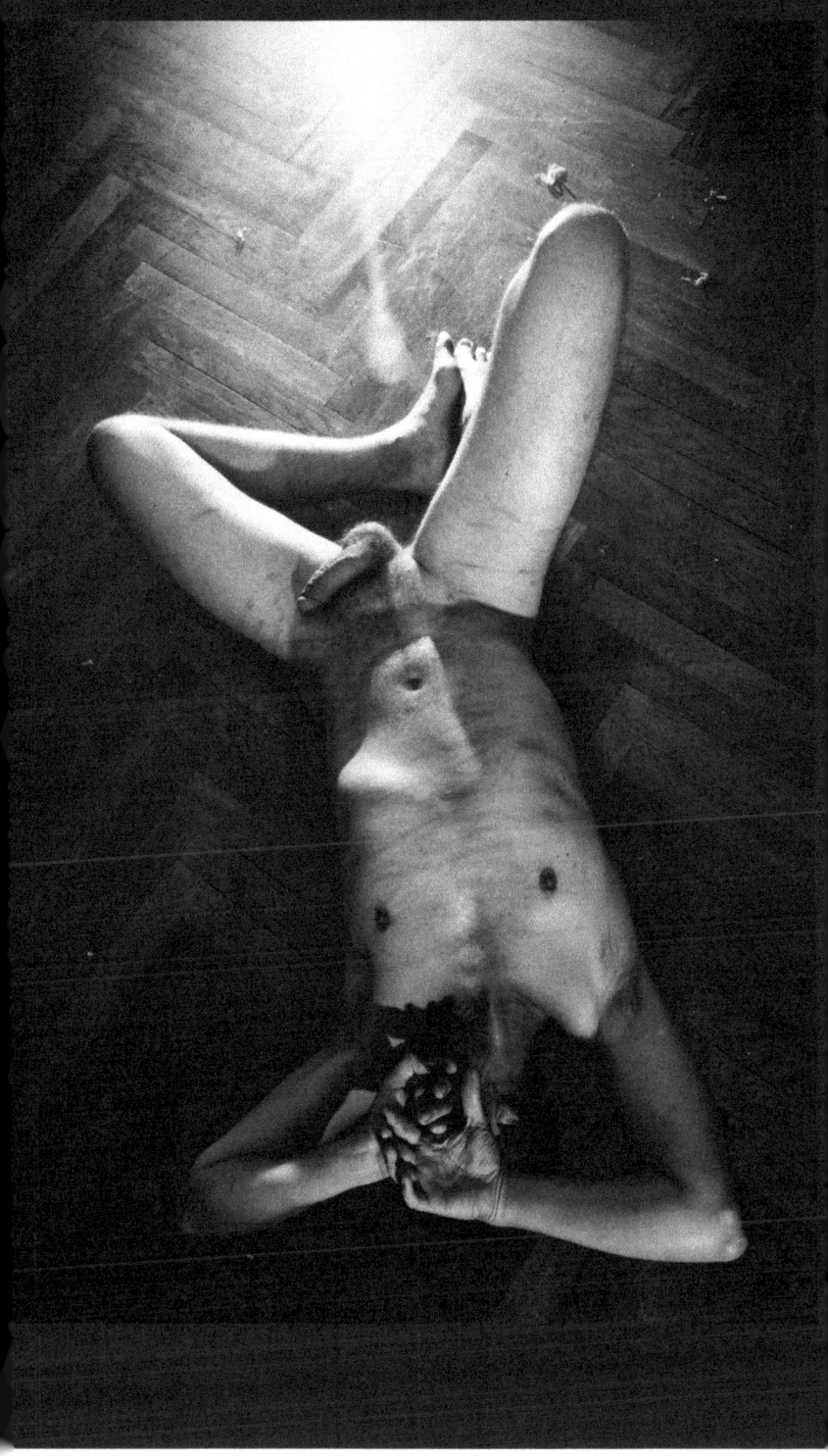

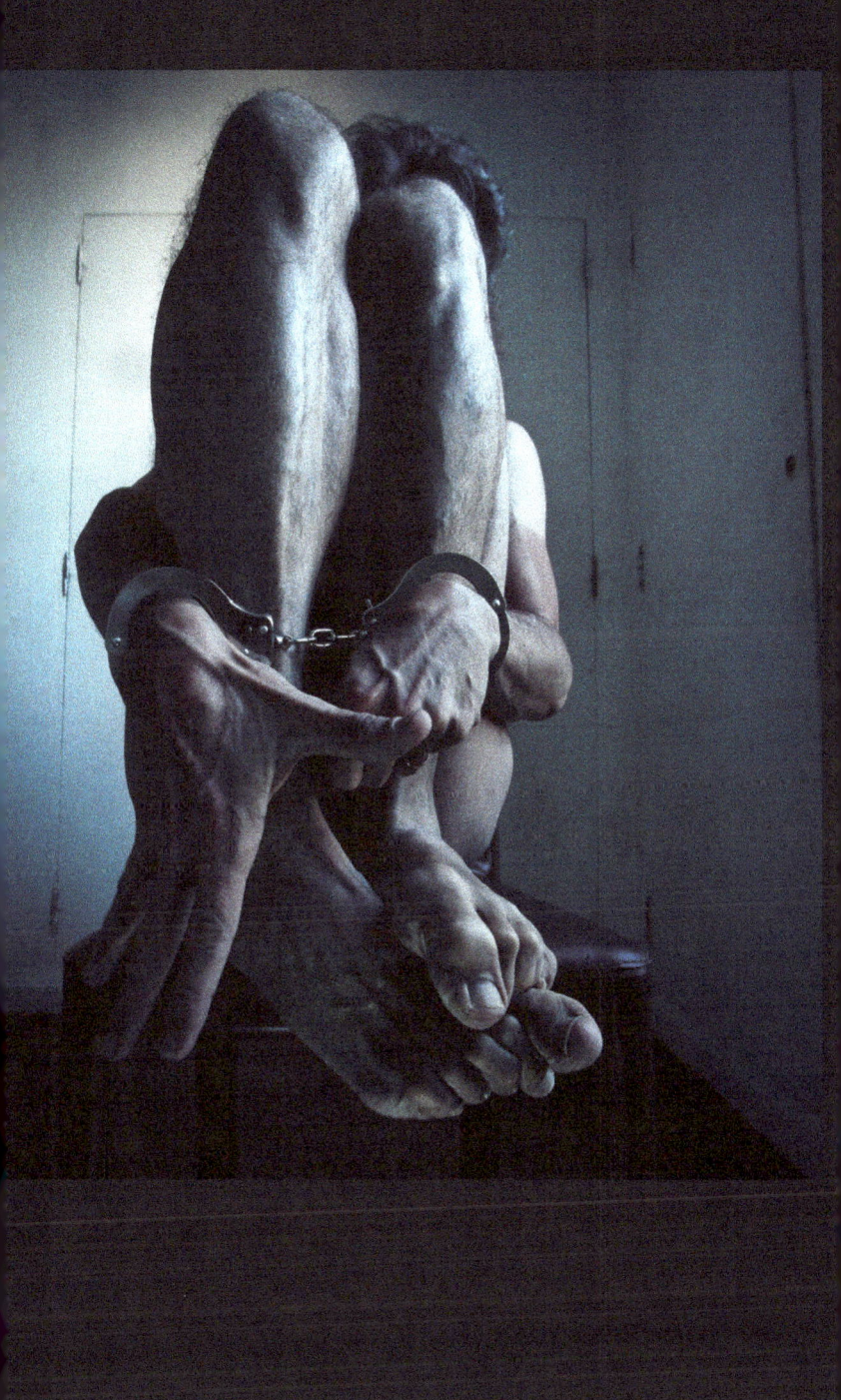

CPSIA information can be obtained
at www.ICGtesting.com
Printed in the USA
BVHW091011200319
543198BV00016B/340/P